KT-372-312

Rubbish and Recycling

by Helen Orme

BAINTE DEN STOC

WITHDRAWN FROM
DÚN LAOGHAIRE-RATHDOWN COUNTY
LIBRARY STOCK

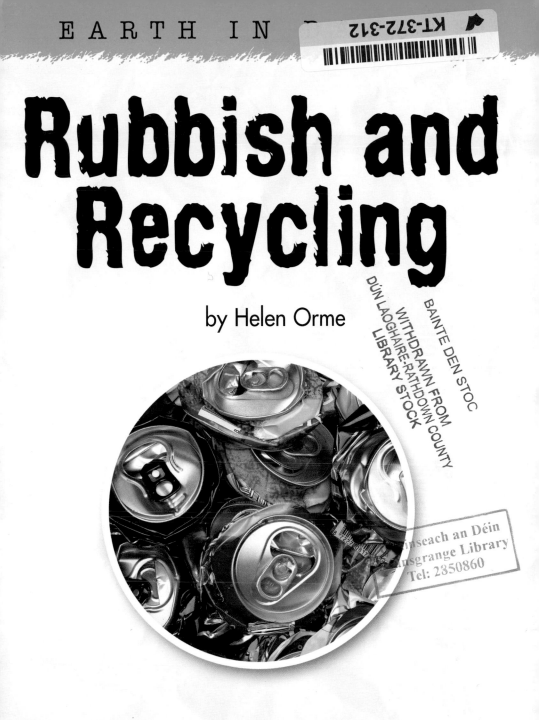

inseach an Déin
nsgrange Library
Tel: 2850860

ticktock

By Helen Orme

Series consultant: Terry Jennings

ticktock editor: Sophie Furse

ticktock designer: Hayley Terry

Picture research: Lizzie Knowles

With thanks to: Joe Harris, Mark Sachner and Claire Lucas

Copyright © ticktock Entertainment Ltd 2008
First published in Great Britain in 2008 by ticktock Media Ltd,
Unit 2, Orchard Business Centre, North Farm Road,
Tunbridge Wells, Kent, TN2 3XF

ISBN 978 1 84696 737 5 pbk
Printed in China

A CIP catalogue record for this book is available from the British Library.
All rights reserved. No part of this publication may be reproduced, copied, stored in a retrieval system
or transmitted in any form or by any means electronic, mechanical, photocopying, recording or
otherwise without prior written permission of the copyright owner.

Picture credit
Don Bayley/ iStock: 29t. BrandX/ SuperStock: 22-23. Image Source/ Photolibrary Group: 12-13. Alexander Hafemann/
iStock: 5t. iStock: 16-17. Jayfish/ Alamy: 15. Moodboard/ Photolibrary Group: 10. Johannes Norporth/ iStock: 2. David
Noton/ Getty Images: 14. Profimedia International s.r.o/ Alamy: 18. Louie Psihoyos/ Corbis: 28b. Rex Features: 21.
Shutterstock: 1, 4-5, 8-9, 9b, 12b, 13b, 19, 20, 24t, 24b, 27b, 29b, 30, 31b, 32, OBC. Stockbyte/ Photolibrary Group: 22b.
Art Wager/ iStock: 27t. Rachel Weill/ Jupiter Images: 25b. Stephen Wilkes/ Getty Images: 7. Sam Yeh/AFP/Getty Images:
OFC.
Every effort has been made to trace the copyright holders, and we apologise in advance for any unintentional omissions.
We would be pleased to insert the appropriate acknowledgements in any subsequent edition of this publication.

CONTENTS

Words that appear **in bold** are explained in the glossary.

TOO MUCH RUBBISH!

*Every day we throw things away. After you finish reading a magazine, you probably throw it in the bin. Many things we buy come in **packaging**, like cans, boxes and bottles. This ends up in the rubbish, too.*

On average, each person in the United Kingdom throws away about 2.7 kilograms of rubbish each day. The rubbish that people in the UK throw away in just two hours would fill the Royal Albert Hall! Making that much rubbish is a problem for our planet.

PROBLEMS FOR OUR PLANET

The rubbish we throw away may contain harmful chemicals and other **pollutants**. Rotting food produces **methane** gas, a **greenhouse gas** that traps heat in our atmosphere, and adds to **global warming**. Global warming may cause severe flooding, because of the melting of the polar ice caps, and extreme weather conditions.

WHAT DO WE THROW AWAY?

What kinds of things end up in the bin?
About one-third of what we throw away is paper
and cardboard. Most of this is made up of
newspapers, magazines and packaging.

About one-fifth of what we throw away is **organic waste** that will rot. Food waste is an important part of this. Trees, flowers and other plants also rot. The rest of our rubbish is mostly made up of plastic, glass, metal and old clothes (fabric).

Most of these things don't need to be thrown away. We can **recycle** or reuse them.

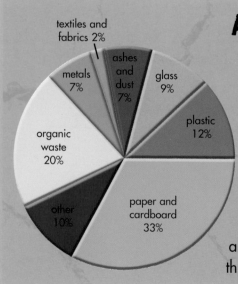

textiles and fabrics 2%
metals 7%
ashes and dust 7%
glass 9%
plastic 12%
organic waste 20%
other 10%
paper and cardboard 33%

A LOOK AT WHAT WE THROW AWAY

The kind of rubbish we throw away has changed over time. In the 1930s, 60% of this pie chart would have been made up of ashes thrown away after coal and wood were burned for heat and fuel. Today, they are only about 7% of what we throw away.

6

If we don't reuse or recycle things, they will end up on a landfill site like this one.

WHY RECYCLE?

Recycling means turning all this rubbish into something useful. This is important for many reasons.

First of all, we are running out of places to put all our rubbish! Much of what we throw away is buried in holes in the ground called **landfills**. We will eventually run out of places to bury our rubbish, however.

There are limited amounts of some **resources**, such as oil and metal. If we continue to take these out of the ground, one day they will run out. So we need to find ways to recycle and reuse these materials.

For both of these reasons it makes sense to turn rubbish into new products instead of throwing it away.

Each of these colourful bins recycles different kind of rubbish: newspapers, plastic, glass and metal cans.

RECYCLING PLASTIC = SAVING OIL

Plastic is made from oil, which is brought to the surface by drills such as the one shown here. Many scientists believe there will not be much oil left 50 years from now.

A machine for recycling metal cans.

 # RECYCLING EVERYDAY THINGS

Almost everything can be recycled in factories like the one shown here. There are many recycled things already in your home, such as newspapers, glass bottles and jars, and plastic containers.

More than 30% of the paper used to print newspapers is recycled. Most of the cardboard used in packaging has also been used before.

Glass can be melted down and turned into new products again and again. This is much cheaper than making new glass. Most glass bottles and jars contain some recycled glass.

Many kinds of plastic can also be recycled. Recycled plastic can be used in many different products, such as raincoats, shopping bags, and window frames.

ORGANIC WASTE

Rubbish that will rot is called organic waste. It may be food waste, grass or garden clippings. This can be recycled too.

Almost one-third of the food we buy ends up in the bin! Some of this is peelings and trimmings from vegetables, and things that we don't normally eat such as bones from meat. However, we could reduce food waste by saving leftovers and not buying more food than we need.

Some kinds of organic waste, such as vegetable peelings, can be left to rot in special containers. After a while, the waste turns into **compost**. Compost can be added to soil to make plants grow more easily.

Egg shells and tea bags can also be composted.

Organic waste from your kitchen can help new food grow in a vegetable patch!

SEWAGE POWER

Even **sewage**, the stuff you flush down the toilet, can be recycled! Once it has been treated in a special way, it can be used as fertiliser on farmland. It can also be burned, and the energy produced from burning sewage can be used to create electricity.

People handling dangerous waste must wear special protective clothing.

WHAT CAN'T WE RECYCLE?

Not all kinds of waste can be recycled. It is hard to recycle different kinds of rubbish if they are mixed together.

Paper covered with food scraps can't be used to make new paper. So don't mix **recyclables** with non-recyclables.

Some packaging mixes plastic and metal. If the two different kinds of waste cannot be separated, they cannot be recycled.

Crisp packets which are made of plastic and metal cannot be recycled.

Some chemical waste from factories is too dangerous and difficult to recycle. However, even rubbish like this doesn't have to end up in a landfill or dumped in places where it might cause harm. There are safe ways to burn this rubbish, and the heat produced can be used to make electricity.

MAKING RECYCLING BETTER

In the past it was hard to recycle some kinds of waste. Plastic was difficult to recycle because there are many different types. Now machines in recycling plants are able to separate them. This means that old plastic bottles can easily be turned into new ones, or other useful products!

Cars, fridges, washing machines and computers are hard and expensive to recycle because they are made from many different plastics and metals. Each type has to be recycled in a different way. Many companies are working on ways to make their new products easier to recycle.

All these fridges are waiting to be recycled.

This special recycling lorry has a crane to lift bottle banks.

TRANSPORT AND RECYCLING

Most towns have recycling centres where you can take plastic, glass, metal, and paper for recycling. In many places, workers collect recyclables from outside your home.

The rubbish for recycling is then transported to plants where different machines deal with different types of recyclables.

Unfortunately, the recycling plants may be hundreds of kilometres away, and the lorries that transport rubbish for recycling are powered by fossil fuels that give off polluting gases.

If the machines that recycle these materials were made smaller, local plants could be set up close to people's homes. It would not be necessary to transport the material so far, and less pollution would be created.

These cans are all ready to be recycled.

RECYCLING AROUND THE WORLD

Rubbish is sometimes transported across the world so it can be recycled in other nations. This picture shows a recycling plant in China. Most of the plastic here comes from Europe or North America.

Many people say it doesn't make sense to ship these materials all around the world. They say it causes too much pollution.

A ship transporting rubbish for recycling.

Others disagree. They say that ships bringing products to Europe and North America from China would return to China empty, so it makes sense to fill them up with used plastic objects. This plastic can then be recycled in China to make things in the factories there.

This Chinese worker in Nanhai is sorting through different kinds of plastics for recycling.

HOW CAN YOU MAKE A DIFFERENCE?

When it comes to rubbish, remember the three 'R's: reduce, reuse, recycle.

Try to reduce how much rubbish you and your family produce. For example, next time you go to the supermarket, ask for reusable bags, and make sure you take them again on your next trip. They can be recycled when they are worn out.

Before you put anything in the bin, ask yourself if you could reuse it instead.

Try to recycle as much of your rubbish as possible. Recycling causes some pollution, but it is much better for the **environment** than sending things to landfills.

Remember to separate your recycling into paper, plastic, glass and metal. If different types of material are mixed up, they cannot be recycled.

LANDFILL

In the past, most rubbish was dumped into huge holes in the ground called landfills. Landfills are still used, but there are many problems with them:

• Any dangerous materials in a landfill, like chemicals from old mobile phone batteries, can seep into the ground. This can get into the water supply and make people who live nearby ill.

Don't just throw away old mobile phones.

• If food waste is put in a landfill, it produces large amounts of methane. Methane is a greenhouse gas that traps the Sun's heat in Earth's atmosphere, adding to global warming.

This landfill site will be grassed over when it is full of rubbish.

• Landfills are often full of materials that could be recycled into something else.

• We are running out of places for landfills.

MAKE YOUR OWN COMPOST

It's easy to make compost from your food and garden waste. If you add compost to the soil in your garden, your plants will grow faster and be healthier.

What to put in your composting bin:

- Peelings from fruits and vegetables, tea bags, egg shells.

- Weeds, prunings and grass cutting.

- Some crumpled waste paper and tissues, but not too much.

What not to put in your composting bin:

- Meat scraps or any cooked food.

- Thick branches or roots from the garden.

- Anything that has just been sprayed with chemicals.

- It's a good idea to stir the mixture each time you add new waste. In six to nine months, your compost will be ready to use! Mix the finished compost into your soil.

You can buy a compost bin, or make your own like this out of recycled wood.

MAKING ELECTRICITY FROM RUBBISH

It's possible to use rubbish to make energy. How does it work?

1. All sorts of waste are put into a landfill site, including rubbish from homes, offices and factories.

2. As the waste rots, it releases gas. About 60% of this gas is made up of methane.

3. A system of pipes under the ground collects the gas, and carries it to a special plant.

4. Inside the plant, the methane is burned as fuel in an engine. As it burns, it creates a hot, fast-moving gas called carbon dioxide. This fast-moving gas makes the engine turn.

5. As the engine turns, it also turns a machine called a generator. As the generator turns, it produces electricity.

REUSE OR RECYCLE?

In the past, glass bottles for milk, soft drinks and beer were reused. They were collected, cleaned, and filled again.

Now most glass bottles are used only once and then recycled. Then they can be melted and turned into new bottles.

What are the advantages of reusing?

• Reusing bottles saves on the energy needed to make new ones. This means less pollution.

• Reusing bottles means we don't have to use fresh materials to make them.

Different coloured glass bottles must be recycled separately.

So why don't we do this?

• Collecting, sorting, transporting and cleaning bottles uses a lot of energy.

• Bottles are easily damaged and can only be used a few times. The average milk bottle can be used about 12 times.

Bottle recycling bins.

• Bottles for reuse have to be stronger than bottles used only once, and so they use more materials.

Whether we decide to recycle or reuse, we should never simply throw glass away!

27

FROM PLASTIC TO FANTASTIC

Plastic bottles and containers will often have recycling information on the label. This tells you what sort of plastic they are made from.

Bottles with the word 'PET' and a number '1' in a triangle are used for soft drinks and many other things. This plastic can be recycled into more bottles, or even into clothes!

If you see the letters 'HDPE' on the container, and a number '2' in a triangle, this harder plastic can be recycled to make things like more bottles, signposts, garden furniture – even hula hoops!

PVC is a very strong plastic. Look for the letters 'V' or 'PVC' and the number '3' in a triangle. This can be recycled to make drainpipes, electrical cables and plugs.

A factory worker inspecting plastic bottles.

DEALING WITH DANGEROUS WASTE

Some waste materials are very dangerous. They must be dealt with in a way that protects people and the environment.

A special bin for hospital waste.

• Hospital waste, such as dirty bandages or medicine containers, might spread disease or contain dangerous drugs.

• Dangerous chemicals from factories and waste from hospitals are burnt in a special way so that no dangerous gases are released into the environment.

• **Radioactive** waste from nuclear power stations cannot be burnt. The only way to safely deal with it is to store it somewhere secure, maybe for thousands of years – usually underground.

Waste from this nuclear power station needs to be stored carefully.

HOW YOU CAN HELP

• Find out about all the materials that can be recycled and make a display at your school.

• Some items, like computer printer cartridges and old mobile phones, can be collected and sent to charities that support all sorts of good causes.

• You can save money by recycling! Instead of buying a present or card, make one out of recycled materials from home.

• Does your home or school have a garden? Get composting!

• Going shopping? Don't just use plastic bags from the shops and then throw them away! Take bags that can be used again.

Visit these websites for more information about rubbish and recycling.

Recyclezone: www.recyclezone.org.uk

Recycle-More: www.recycle-more.co.uk

The Recycle Now Campaign: www.recyclenow.com

The Recycling Guide: www.recycling-guide.org.uk

GLOSSARY

compost Natural material that has rotted and can be added to the soil to improve it.

environment An area or place – including climate, living conditions, and types of life forms in that area – where people, plants, and animals live.

fertiliser Food for plants, which helps them to grow.

global warming The warming of the planet's air and oceans as a result of a build-up of greenhouse gases in the atmosphere.

greenhouse gases Gases like carbon dioxide and methane that help warm the planet by preventing heat from escaping from the atmosphere into space.

landfills Big holes in the ground that serve as dumping areas for rubbish.

methane A gas given off when material rots. It can be burned to give heat to make electricity.

packaging Glass, plastic, paper and metal materials used to wrap goods that are for sale.

organic waste Material that once was living matter, including food, plants, animal remains, or human and animal waste.

pollutants Harmful substances that are released into the environment.

radioactive When something sends out radiation which causes dangerous changes in living things.

recyclables Objects made out of material that can be recycled and reused.

recycle To turn unwanted materials into something useful.

resources Everything we need for life, such as water, food, fuel and energy.

sewage Liquid and solid waste matter carried away by pipes and drains.

INDEX